# Birth Control, INSURANCE COVERAGE, & the Religious Right

### By A.F. Alexander

I0171230

**Blazing Sword Publishing Ltd.**

Colorado Springs, CO

For information, address Blazing Sword
Publishing Ltd.
http://www.blazingswordpub.com

For more information or to book an event,
please refer to the author's website at
religiousright101.com.

Library of Congress: Pending

ISBN-13: 978-0615778686

1 – Women's Studies
2 – Current Events
3 – Religion

Birth Control, Insurance Coverage, and the Religious Right

A.F. Alexander

# Contents

A.F. Alexander

# Introduction

In 2012, the Catholic Church strategically chose to make an issue about insurance coverage for the most common hormonal birth control, for any of their female employees. This controversy is still raging as lawsuits have been filed, and politicians pontificate.

The issue of an organized religion attempting to impose their views on a third party -- insurance companies -- is far-reaching. The government requires certain types of insurance coverage, as we see in mandatory car insurance with minimum coverage. But for an employer, albeit one of the world's largest churches, to tell a third party what they can or cannot not offer in coverage is an old world manifestation that was seen in the Dark Ages with church control over every facet of life.

Remember all the objections to the Affordable Care Act and how the scare-tactic was used that government would be between you and your doctor? Imagine an employer between you, your doctor, and your insurance coverage, dictating what a third party insurance company can even offer a woman.

I briefly addressed the birth control coverage outrage in the book <u>Religious Right: The Greatest Threat to Democracy</u> (see further information about the book at the end of this booklet.) But there was far more that needed covering, so I wrote a series of articles, in addition to the book. I believe they are more effective as an unbroken discussion, so I have brought them together here and have added to them. The articles are presented in a seamless manner, and an entirely new chapter has been added that addresses an additional perspective.

In Chapter 1, we examine the often-overlooked reality of this issue of elevating an employer's conscience to the same status as individuals', and claiming First Amendment coverage. This is a reinforcement of the Citizens United decision, that will be covered in more detail.

The premise that providing birth control is paying for a woman's promiscuity is a lie. We cover the lies and distortions of the issue in Chapter 2.

Legally, how will allowing a church entity to be exempt, or above, federal laws impact our legal system as this trend goes forward? In Chapter 3, we cover the disastrous results of such a decision, in the repercussions that could seriously impact women's rights in our society.

In this scenario, the individual woman is being forced out of the equation, as though a woman's concerns and conscience are irrelevant. We cover that topic in Chapter 4, about how pharmacy technicians' and emergency room workers' blatant refusal to provide birth control is spreading, and we explore the ramifications of those conscientious objections.

# Birth Control, Insurance Coverage, and the Religious Right

"No, you can't deny women their basic rights and pretend it's about your 'religious freedom.' If you don't like birth control, don't use it. Religious freedom doesn't mean you can force others to live by your beliefs."
Barack Obama, 44th President of the United States of America

# Chapter 1
# The Citizens United of Religious Liberty

Citizens United made history. Fifty years ago, it would have been hard to imagine that a business entity could claim individual constitutional rights. However, in the wake of Citizens United being granted freedom of speech rights, corporations effectively equate to people, under the law. That a legal and tax status, such as the incorporation of a business, could ensure it the same inalienable rights that our Declaration of Independence provides to citizens, and that our Constitution protects, is still hard to fathom. Ever since the Supreme Court upheld Citizens United, many average Americans have disliked it and began efforts to counter it, including talk of a Constitutional Amendment that would effectively block the high court's ruling.

Perhaps that is such old news that nobody blinks when a similarly epic twisting of priorities -- the elevating of employer/corporate rights as superior to individual religious liberty -- made headlines. First, the Catholic Church (in May 2012 there were 40+ Catholic agencies in the U.S.) and businesses such as Hobby Lobby were asserting their "rights," as collective or corporate entities, to determine the personal health coverage they would allow. This is the equivalent of the Citizens United ruling, that relegates individual religious conscience and rights as inferior to an organized body's, or business entity's. It is not as if this is happening in back-rooms with stealthy moves. Rather, it is splashed on television news, radio, print, and even Facebook.

This issue has continued to create headlines, most recently because Wheaton College joined with Catholic University in a lawsuit to fight providing standard, common birth control coverage for employees. Initially, the Catholic Church's protests inspired more widespread, sweeping denial of health coverage beyond just birth control, as witnessed in the Blunt Amendment. This amendment declared that making *any* business provide any kind of health coverage that a business entity had a conscientious objection to, was a violation of that company's rights. Fortunately, it did not pass the Senate. Recently, Tyndale Publishing House picked up that particular banner and now protests covering "abortion pills" as a for-profit corporation, unlike the handfuls of 501c3 non-profits that began the uproar.

On August 1, 2012, the Christian Post published poll results that claim fifty-six percent of Catholics who specifically heard of the controversy sided with the Bishop's claim of a violation to the *church's* religious liberty. The Christian Post didn't break the poll respondents into male/female categories, however.

When birth control insurance coverage first became a national controversy, I spoke to several of my Catholic lady friends and acquaintances. I was surprised at the number of professional, independent, and intelligent women who didn't think about their personal religious freedom and rights in the matter. Rather, they deferred to the Church's rights, without a thought to the limiting of their freedom of religious expression and choice – even if they personally took birth control. But, one of my friends was so disturbed by this mandate over women, and other pulpit politics from her life-long family denomination, that she considered facing family outrage and leaving the Catholic church. Initially, she turned to her parish priest and implored him for a reason to stay, an explanation that might soothe her feelings of betrayal. Rather, she received steadfast dogma and not one ounce of understanding. My friend went through a crisis of faith due to this. She broke completely with the Catholic Church and joined a less political Protestant church.

I then turned to Catholic women's groups for statements. The National Council of Catholic Women in the U.S. did not reply to my inquiry. The Association of Catholic Women in the United Kingdom *did* answer my email, with a standard statement deferring to the Church's rights and the perceived assault on religious liberty – without a hint of individual rights in general, nor women's religious rights in particular. *"...despite employers' conscientious objections to such treatments on religious grounds, appears to us to be a direct contravention of the First Amendment's guarantee of freedom of religion. Freedom of religion is simply incompatible with any restriction on the citizens' right to live and*

11

*conduct his affairs in accordance with the teachings of his religion."* This clearly equates an employer's conscience (a business entity) to a person's religious liberty.

The first sentence gives First Amendment coverage to employers, and the second sentence talks of a citizen's right to conduct his (or her) affairs and to live, not as they personally believe – **but as their employer requires**. There is no recognition that the very concept of religious liberty has been redefined to elevate corporate identity to personhood, claiming First Amendment coverage. Nor is there recognition that they have replaced citizens' rights to live as *they personally believe,* with following *their church -- or employer's* beliefs. Let us remember, many people who are employed by the Catholic church are not necessarily Catholic themselves, especially in this economy when a job is a valuable commodity. But as an employer, the church can enforce a corporate belief structure on all their employees, rather than leaving the option to individual beliefs. Those are two very different concepts. Personal religious liberty is over-ruled in favor of a corporate church's dictates on congregants' lives. This results in the individual's right to choose based on his/her own convictions being stomped into the dust in favor of an employer's conscience -- with none of the furor that Citizens United continually experiences.

This further institutionalizes business entities as persons. We are witnessing a massive shifting away from the religious liberty of the person and squarely with a church or business entity, and yet few seem to recognize it as such. Why don't more people see the birth control insurance coverage outrage for what it -- is, corporate rights trumping individual liberty?

"Put into perspective, the concept that a woman isn't fulfilling her God-ordained role of a 'home working' wife or celibate daughter, then she is shaking her fist at God's sovereignty and at the divine order of the universe. The woman who goes against God's clear definition of her only role is out of God's favor. She is being selfish at best, and sinful at worst." A.F. Alexander, <u>Religious Right: The Greatest Threat to Democracy</u>, Blazing Sword Publishing, Ltd., 2012.

# Chapter 2
# Religious Right Controlling the Birth Control Argument

No matter what the federal and state election results, the Religious Right and "Values Voters" will be relentless in their continual attack on abortion and the use of birth control. It seems amazing that we have to fight for basic birth control to be fully covered by insurance in this day-and-age. But yet, here we are.

Birth control is and was the biggest singular event for women's liberation. It allowed women to take control of their destinies by delaying starting a family. This allowed women to focus on education and a career, and even to solidify marriages before children were introduced. *"Our country's top health agency, the Centers for Disease Control and Prevention, counts contraception as one of the 10 greatest health achievements of the 20th century.... Demonizing it amounts to telling these women to throw out their briefcases and take up their vacuum cleaners.*" Laura Sessions Stepp, "Anti-science and anti-contraception," <u>CNN Opinion</u>, May 22, 2012. It is the pill's role as the great liberator of women that is most significant for our purposes.

In 1873, the Comstock Law was passed, that equated birth control to pornography, and thus it became illegal to even reference birth control methods to be distributed or mailed. Connecticut had an 1879 law still on the books and enforced against anything that prevented conception as illegal. In 1965, Estelle Griswold was arrested based on this moldy law. The arrest was appealed all the way to the Supreme Court and the case was argued on the basis of the privacy of married couples and the Fourteenth Amendment. When the Supreme Court ruled in favor of Estelle Griswold, it effectively made it legal to obtain birth control for married couples. Eventually the ruling covered unmarried couples as well.

When the pill is put into the perspective of its historical significance as the great liberator of women, what does the outrage over its coverage in health care really tell us? This outrage we are witnessing is because many view the liberation of women as a bad event. The Religious Right like to blame women entering the work force as the sole reason that wages across the board have stagnated, rather than executive and CEO greed for more profit. I have heard such blaming of women from the pulpit. I have even heard it preached that the pill is responsible for the decline of marriage and rise of divorce rates.

> *"The Food and Drug Administration approved the first pill in the first year of the Swinging Sixties, but the pill did not spark the sexual revolution. Nor did it*

17

*cause a sudden drop in the U.S. fertility rate, which didn't bottom out until the early 1970s....*

*It became a symbol of women's rights and generational change — and, for a time, the focus of a debate over whether it led to declining morals....*

*'The charge in the 1960s was that the pill was responsible for the sexual revolution,' [Andrea] Tone says. 'It was relaxing moral standards. ... It was promoting promiscuity.' Yet, she notes, a 1953 Kinsey report on female sexual behavior — released years before the pill became available — found that half of all women had premarital sex.*

*By 1967, the pill merited a Time magazine cover story.... 'Does the convenient contraceptive promote promiscuity?' Time asked. 'In some cases, no doubt it does — as did the automobile, the drive-in movie and the motel. But the consensus among both physicians and sociologists is that a girl who is promiscuous on the pill would have been promiscuous without it.'"* Rita Robin, "The pill: 50 years of birth control changed women's lives," USA Today, May 8, 2010.

The righteous indignation over abortion is now strategically and deliberately directed towards birth control. Birth control pills are being falsely marketed as a chemical abortion, "abortifacient," claiming that they chemically force the uterine wall to reject a fertilized egg. But in fact, "the pill mimics the hormone profile of pregnant and lactating women..." according to Malcolm Potts' article, "A contraception game-changer" in The Los Angeles Times online, February 20, 2012. What if the war against abortion had always had the end-goal of turning that outrage against the pill to legislate women back into the home, barefoot and pregnant? Makes you think.

## The Religious Right defines and controls the discussion by shaming women

The Religious Right has manufactured a scandal over full birth control coverage in insurance plans. They have successfully manufactured this outrage because they have controlled the argument and kept it focused on non-issues. It is a successful smear campaign because they use the following tactics to shame women.

The Religious Right has twisted health insurance coverage of commonly used birth control into paying for, and condoning, promiscuity. *"But what if free birth control just makes women into sluts? Jeanne Monahan of the anti-abortion Family Research Council told the AP that contraceptive use might make people have so much more sex that -- since contraception sometimes doesn't work -- there will actually be more unwanted pregnancies.*" Erika Eichelberger, "Shocker: Free Birth Control Means Fewer Abortions," <u>Mother Jones</u>, October 5, 2012.

Never mind that taxpayers do not cover the costs, as many mistakenly believe. Viagra, Cialis and other male erectile dysfunction medications are commonly covered by insurance plans, but there is no promiscuity stigma associated with them. The double standard is blatant, and unapologetic. Men must be able to have their sex, while leaving all the responsibility and the "slut-factor" with women.

It is astonishing that the campaign to label the pill as being for sluts has been successful among some women as well. But consider that many instances of pharmacy workers refusing to do their jobs and fill birth control prescriptions impacted married women with their husbands by their sides. Are we returning to the bad ole' days of woman being thought of as evil if they enjoy sex, and yet men are cheered for their conquests? It certainly seems to be the case, when so many politicians who run "faith and family values" campaigns are exposed for having mistresses without much outrage, but yet when one college student who attempts to testify on behalf of birth control insurance coverage is publicly vilified and ridiculed. The notion that such hypocritical double standards were left behind in the nostalgic fifties appears to be incorrect.

They also have worked hard to make contraception -- the pill specifically -- a moral dilemma. The pill is now called an abortifacient, essentially claiming it is a chemical abortion, and they desire the same human rights protection to a fertilized egg --

mostly as an attempt to overturn the Roe vs. Wade decision.

The shaming of women has become the standard manner to address reproductive issues. When forced vaginal probes became acceptable, we as a nation sanctioned government-sponsored rape to not just defile, but shame any woman seeking to terminate a pregnancy. In a prison, it would be called rape, but now that it is state mandated, people justify the violation as if the woman deserves it. Thus, we see even local governments participating in widespread and systematic shaming of women to shut them up.

Distraction from the real issues

The third way the Religious Right is framing the discussion is by distracting from the real issue of women's health and equality. The notorious "legitimate rape" comments spouted by Religious Right Missouri

Representative Todd Akin have been discounted as simply a case of pseudo-science. While science is not popular among the Religious Right, let's be clear on what Mr. Akin was saying by using the phrase "legitimate rape." He and other Religious Right politicians are referring to Deut 22:23-27 that draws a clear distinction between a "valid," "legitimate," and "forced rape" versus a frivolous accusation because the woman got caught or is pregnant. That is the actual message behind Akin's statement that has largely slipped under the radar. This is soft-selling the promiscuity accusation, but does double duty by misdirecting the argument by alleging that "in-fact," "forcible rape" is not that common.

The pseudo science of miraculously avoiding pregnancy is what got the attention, not that Akin and the Religious Right discounted and cast suspicion on all rapes as being a manipulative crying wolf. It alludes to women falsely claiming rape just to get that "morning after pill" or an abortion to avoid consequences for their promiscuity -- again. The old attitude that a rape victim probably deserved the attack is back with a vengeance, too. Wisconsin State Rep. Roger Rivard, endorsed by Religious-Righter Paul Ryan, stated "some girls rape easy." Rep. Rivard tried damage control by claiming he was referring to his father's advice that consensual sex becomes rape if girls are attempting to avoid consequences, so you can't trust them. The explanation dug his hole deeper, but amazingly his campaign thought it would make the situation better. Not surprisingly, Vice Presidential candidate Paul Ryan actually co-sponsored H.R. 3, the "No Taxpayer Funding for Abortion Act," that demanded the only exception allowing for an abortion was in cases of "forcible rape."

Another aspect of this shell-game distraction is exemplified in the headlines regarding high profile Planned Parenthood. Planned Parenthood has recently fended off attacks and attempts to terminate funding by repeatedly asserting their many health services for women, like mammograms, other cancer screenings, and low-cost contraception pills. Perhaps the best-kept secret in this discrediting of birth control is how the pill has documented scientific-endorsed health benefits. This article's excerpt explains the very clear health benefits of the pill for women, and challenge the Catholic Church as an added bonus:

> *"Several years ago, British medical scientists published a 39-year follow-up of 23,000 women who started using the pill in the 1960s and 23,000 who did not. Among pill users, they found a significant reduction in ovarian, uterine*

*and bowel cancers, and even melanomas. Another study of 17,000 women found that use of the pill was associated with a small but measurable increase in life expectancy.*

*Last December, at the Pontifical University of the Holy Cross in Vatican City, two Australian scientists, Kara Britt and Roger Short, gave a keynote address titled 'The Plight of Nuns.' They recommended that nuns should take the pill for a couple of years during their lifetimes to reduce the increased risk of cancer associated with not having children. It was not a tongue-in-cheek criticism of the Vatican but good medical advice based on impeccable statistics and sound biological insights. It was also theologically sound.*

*The pill was first marketed in the 1950s not as a contraceptive but to regularize menstruation, and Pope Pius XII approved this use of the drug."* Malcolm Potts, "A contraception game-changer," <u>Los Angeles Times</u> online, February 20, 2012.

We must stand together, united behind the actual issue of women's access to effective health care and take back the argument. No more misdirecting from the actual issue of legislating women back into the home by limiting, perhaps ultimately eliminating, the single greatest liberator of women -- the birth control pill.

*"'Be fruitful and multiply' ... is a command of God, indeed the first command to a married couple. Birth control obviously involves disobedience to this command, for birth control attempts to prevent being fruitful and multiplying. Therefore birth control is wrong, because it involves disobedience to the Word of*

*God. Nowhere is this command done away with in the entire <u>Bible</u>; therefore it still remains valid for us today."* Charles D. Provan, <u>The Bible and Birth Control</u>, Zimmer, June, 1989.

Is it too much to ask that women can stand together on this issue? Birth control and family planning are not evil, but responsible, and exhibit good stewardship. The facts must be faced, that the pill is better than the increasing teen pregnancy rates under the failed "abstinence only" school programs. Basic birth control pills should be fully covered as preventative medicine. It is about women's health, and their liberation – AGAIN, before we wake up one morning back in the bad ole' days.

*"Birth control has been illegal or restricted for longer than it has been legal in this country." A.F. Alexander, <u>Religious Right: The Greatest Threat to Democracy</u>, Blazing Sword Publishing, Ltd., 2012.*

# Chapter 3
# Dangerous precedent: Religious exemption from federal law

<u>What is a precedent and how important is it?</u>

A precedent is a court case's legal decision that may be used as a standard in subsequent, similar cases. Roe vs. Wade set a legal precedent, and because of that court decision, abortion became legal. Prior court case decisions are cited often in legal cases to demonstrate that their side is already on established ground and thus should win.

The approaching birth control-insurance coverage showdown will set a precedent that could dramatically shape this country in the future. The legal precedent that may be set has some serious ramifications that have gone largely unconsidered. We shall explore a few of those issues in the remainder of this writing.

## Religious exemption from law as a precedent

The Catholic Church has filed legal responses to the requirement for insurance companies to cover the cost of birth control pills (at last count there were well over forty separate legal actions). This is the most common form of contraception and impacts employees of Catholic hospitals and other Catholic enterprises or charities, whether the women are Catholic or not. The Catholic Church is aggressively pushing for a religious exemption from this federal law that impacts a third party, insurance companies, to cover what is considered common preventative care.

## Exempt from other laws

The first precedent, should they get such a religious exemption, is that religious organizations or companies can be exempted from other federal level laws. This is a huge strike against the republic ideal where all citizens, companies, and organizations must comply with the same laws. The Catholic Church considering itself above the law of the land is not a new idea. The Catholic Church in Vatican City is actually, and technically, its own country (not just part of Rome or Italy) with its own laws and separate law enforcement. The Catholic Church expecting special treatment may be in keeping with its view of itself as outside any country's laws, but that doesn't excuse it in America where we expect all to follow the laws of the land. The Catholic church has already inspired other employers, who aren't specifically religious in nature, to insist on special exemptions from the same federal law impacting a third party.

## Creates a special class

In addition to this blow against this country's core democratic republic structure, such a religious exemption to federal law will create a special class of organizations that gets special treatment, which is counter to the First Amendment. Will your average charity get such exemptions from federal laws if they don't agree with a law? Church and religious organizations get special tax-free status. Thus, each individual can give money where he or she chooses, rather than the government showing favor to any particular religion or sect over another. This goes even further by making them so special, that they choose what laws they will or will not accept.

## IRS tax restrictions and the Johnson Amendment

Consider just the core concept of receiving an exemption from laws because of your religious beliefs and how, beyond birth control, far reaching the ripples could be of such a landmark decision. Consider the old case of Bob Jones University that refused admittance to black student applicants until 1975, and afterward only accepted those applicants who were married to a black spouse. They did this according to their religious beliefs against interracial marriage. The IRS revoked their tax-exempt status and Bob Jones fought back. The case, titled Bob Jones University versus United States, held that the IRS was within its rights. This has fostered a seething anger toward the federal government holding such power, tax-free status via federal law adherence, over any Christian institution. The IRS tax exemption codes will likely be the very next in line to be challenged if the precedent of religious exemption from a federal law is allowed. The court decision in Bob Jones University v. United States clearly applies to the same concept, as seen in the following quote.

> *"... entitlement to tax exemption*
> *depends on meeting certain common-law*

*standards of charity – namely that an institution seeking tax-exempt status must serve a public purpose and not be contrary to established public policy. Neither petitioner qualifies as a tax -- exempt organization...[i]t would be wholly incompatible with the concepts underlying tax exemption to grant tax-exempt status to racially discriminatory private educational entities. Whatever may be the rationale for such private schools' policies, racial discrimination in education is contrary to public policy. Racially discriminatory educational institutions cannot be viewed as conferring a public benefit within the above 'charitable' concept or within the congressional intent underlying 501(c)(3)."* Findlaw.com

The racial discrimination exemplified by Bob Jones University that started their long legal battle will easily be challenged once again with the "religious exemption" excuse, depending upon how this birth control coverage challenge is resolved.

Over the last several years, churches have been openly defiant of federal IRS laws that specifically draw the line at endorsing a specific candidate. On Pulpit Freedom Sundays, church leaders band together and become political candidate spokesmen. This year, several churches even video-taped their pulpit politicking in an open challenge to the government. The Pulpit Freedom Sunday website provides a history of the Johnson Amendment that passed Congress in 1954, which defined the political boundaries for tax-free charitable organizations. The organizers and participants of Pulpit Freedom Sunday along with other sympathetic organizations feel the tax code is used against them, rather than benefiting them with billions in tax free

money. The Freedom From Religion
Foundation, a church–state separation
watchdog group, filed a lawsuit against the
IRS for not pursuing this blatant law-breaking
by approximately 1,500 churches this year, and
filed twenty-seven complaints regarding
church politicking throughout 2012. The tax
regulations and the Johnson Amendment will
definitely be one of the first challenged if there
is a precedent of churches being exempt from
federal law based on their beliefs. Count on it.

A potential Mormon challenge

During the 2012 presidential campaign, the
nation learned that some Mormon families
moved to Mexico to escape the marriage laws
that specify only one spouse in the United
States. There are still those of the Mormon
faith who could easily challenge the anti-
bigamy laws with a religious exemption
precedent since multiple wives are part of their

belief system. This situation could get particularly interesting because anti-bigamy was part of our English heritage, based on English common law. It was established because monogamy was the accepted Christian norm, despite the multiple wives of Solomon and King David. So which belief system gets to have its way, or is it just whatever your church believes trumps the laws of the land, and let anarchy reign? This is a legal challenge that could easily take advantage of a religious exemption to laws, claiming their church's well-documented multiple-wife belief-system should be exempt from the prevailing law of the land. You have to wonder if the Mormon Church is already planning their legal strategy if the Catholic Church's present legal challenges should win.

Child brides and child abuse

Warren Jeffs, and the towns of Hilldale, Utah and Colorado City, Arizona provide another excellent example for this discussion. Warren Jeffs is the religious leader of these two towns. A lawsuit filed in 2012 against the city leaders and law enforcement, claims abuse of their powers for following Jeffs' orders above their sworn duties. This was sparked by the 2008 raid of Warren Jeff's Zion Ranch in Texas, which took four hundred children into custody. It became the largest custody case on record in U.S. history.

Warren Jeffs and the towns of Hilldale and Colorado City give perfect examples of religious beliefs that are in direct conflict with the law. There are many instances of child brides in these two towns, a situation that is completely within their leadership's beliefs, if not the girls'. *The town's police are accused of "confronting a sect member to try to return an underage bride to her husband after she fled.... Jeffs is imprisoned in Texas after being found guilty last year of sexually assaulting two of his two dozen underage brides."* Staff Reporter, "Polygamous towns, home to Warren Jeffs cult, sued for destroying homes and properties of non-believers," Daily Mail UK Online, June 22, 2012.

Warren Jeffs and the people of Hilldale, Utah, and Colorado City, Arizona can easily utilize a legal precedent of a religious organization being exempt from the laws of the land. It may seem outlandish to some that the church exemption of birth control coverage on religious grounds could impact these types of cases, but this certainly may be attempted. Child brides are found in a variety of religions around the world, according to the International Center for Research on Women. Thus, there will no doubt be a few churches

41

using the examples of Hilldale and Colorado City to test the new legal precedent of religious exemption in their cases.

Child abuse is another example, because those who believe the Proverbs 13:24 quote "spare the rod and spoil the child," or the example of stoning a rebellious child, give license to the parent for actions that society considers excessive or abusive punishment. Would you care to take any bets as to which will be the first to test the religious exemption from laws first: bigamy, child brides, or child abuse?

Domestic violence

Then, there is the little-talked-about issue of domestic violence within the church. Many Evangelical pastors stand firm that a woman has no biblical grounds to leave an abusive husband. Such a statement was even visible on Rick Warren's Saddleback Church website, until it received media attention. First, note that by addressing that the wife must stay in an abusive situation, they are admitting that they are aware there is a domestic abuse problem in the church membership, i.e. there is enough of a problem to have a policy and to post it. This is still an issue that most don't want to admit is a *problem* in the church, but there are those churches that have in their belief structures that women need to be corrected and even struck, that women must be tightly reigned in, for they are rebellious, like Eve. A domestic violence case may eventually make it to court, utilizing the "religious exemption from laws" precedent. It is more a question of when, not *if,* that defense shall be brought forth.

Worth speaking up

We haven't touched on the many other laws that will probably be challenged, such as the

Hate Crimes Prevention Act, popularly called the Matthew Shepard Act, or even the elimination of the minimum wage requirement, based on Matthew 20:1-16. As you can see, the legal precedent of granting a church or religious organization exemption from a valid law is potentially far-reaching. The ripples from such a decision will undermine the civil order around us, and wear at the fabric of our very society.

In the book <u>Religious Right: The Greatest Threat to Democracy</u>, the desire to take over the court system, control the Supreme Court, and modify our entire legal system to align U.S. laws with <u>Old Testament</u> laws is exposed as a top Religious Right goal. The legal precedent of a religious exemption may topple the U.S. legal system to the point that it can be refashioned to align to the Religious Right's extremist views. The Religious Right has been murderously angry over the losses they have suffered in lawsuits. Could this be a bid to up-end our legal system so they might refashion it to their liking?

It is critical to consider the ramifications these legal challenges based on religion will definitely have. The impacts may appear in ways we could not imagine at this point. This is too high a price, on many grounds. If you care about these issues, please write your state and federal elected officials with these concerns, and write to your newspapers. This is too important for anyone who cares about women's rights to sit by as a spectator.

"*In October of 2008, Chicago hosted the first 'True Woman Conference' with a turn-out of over 6,000 women who affirm 'Biblical Womanhood' and 'the Patriarchy Movement.' Organizers happily proclaim that it is directly counter to the women's liberation movement of the nineteen sixties.*"
A.F. Alexander, <u>Religious Right: The Greatest Threat to Democracy</u>, Blazing Sword Publishing, Ltd., 2012.

# Chapter 4
# Any Objection is More Important than a Woman's

Sex addiction for some male celebrities is now a common news item, perhaps even a trend. There seems to be an outbreak of men who are sex addicts, from Tiger Woods to the former husband of Sandra Bullock, yet health insurance covers Viagra and Cialis without the Catholic Church refusing their male employees to have such coverage. The fact is, it is only the women whose sex-lives are on display that are attacked as evidence of deviance and sinfulness to the point of removing their freedom and liberty. That makes the entire issue of a "conscientious objection" highly subjective and a matter of prejudice and personal bias. Why haven't conscientious objections been scrutinized as a religio-political agenda?

47

*"Likewise, even when the pronatalist, anticontraception motivations of the antiabortion movement are made clear, as when some U.S. pharmacists began refusing to fill birth control prescriptions for unwed women or for any woman who intended to use the pill as contraception, media reports rarely dig into the theological grounding and real-life implications of their arguments. The implication of the anticontraception position is the "Quiverfull" belief system: that women should accept every child as an unconditional blessing and that family planning is immoral. Media coverage has thus far failed to connect the individual pharmacists, portrayed as conscientious objectors standing alone with their religious beliefs, with the growing ranks of anticontraception activists at their back. When I first*

*began looking into the phenomenon of pharmacist refusals in 2004 ... I was shocked to hear the explicitly anti contraception message of the pharmacists' advocates and the deeply antifeminist politics of their allies. I was more surprised to realize the detail and complexity of the antifeminist lifestyle these allies proposed for women in its place and how well the movement was already organized."* Kathryn Joyce, Quiverfull: Inside the Christian Patriarchy Movement, Beacon Press, March, 2009.

Quiverfull is the Religious Right's template for the proper family -- the god-ordained family order. The battle against contraception is bolstered and propelled by Quiverfull advocates. More and more legislation is being proposed, and becoming law, that protects the rights of pharmacy staff to refuse filling a doctor's prescription based on their opinions, with no regard for the woman or consumer's rights. Where is the equal outrage that was stirred up at the thought of the government getting between individuals and their doctors -- when it is a pharmacy worker between a woman and her doctor? Remember the days when such a conscientious objection was an indication that the pharmacy worker needed to change career fields? The Religious Right actually encourages followers to seek out career fields specifically intending the job to be a mission field to witness and impact. In the case of pharmacy workers, it seems to be quite a successful strategy.

May 15, 2012, Kansas Governor Sam Brownback signed a bill into law that protects pharmacy workers who refuse to fill a prescription because of a perceived risk of terminating a pregnancy. This bill protects them from being fired when they refuse to do the job they are hired to do. No more "customer is always right" -- not when the customer is a woman.

> *"Women who already have difficulty obtaining contraception may face additional hurdles, according to Julie Burkhart, founder of an abortion-rights group in Wichita, Kansas:*
>
> *Burkhart said the law could create a **hardship for women in small towns with a sole pharmacist who may refuse to fill certain prescriptions**. In larger cities, women will have to make sure they go to a cooperative pharmacist, she added.*
>
> *'**Women should not have to go armed with a lot of research when looking for a physician or pharmacist** in the community,' Burkhart said."*

Amanda Peterson Beadle,
"Pharmicists In Kansas Can Now
Deny Women Access to Birth
Control," Think Progress, May 16,
2012.

This is becoming more common than in just
Kansas. In fact, this is an epidemic that few
want to talk about because we may actually
have to admit the Religious Right is impacting
our society. The media has minimally covered
this growing phenomenon, likely not realizing
the religio-political agenda actually behind it.
It isn't like Quiverfull is a household name or
well understood for their political plan, even if
the movement's name is known. You may be
questioning what difference extremists
actually make in the big picture? The anti
birth control idea hasn't been taken seriously
in this modern, "post feminist" world, which
enables it to take root with little fight. Some
would say the Catholic Church is just being its

usual bossy self. But consider Pharmacists for Life International, who are organized and have a pledge to sign, or the Pro-Life Pharmacy website and Facebook page as indicators of their determination and growing numbers.

*"Pharmacists in at least 24 states have refused to sell birth control or emergency contraception to women. Some hospital emergency rooms refuse to provide emergency contraception to rape victims.*

*Some healthcare providers even lie to women—for example, by saying it will cause an abortion. In one case, a woman believed a Wisconsin pharmacist who called her a murderer. Although it will not work once a woman is pregnant, she did not fill her prescription and got pregnant. In a California incident, a couple with a newborn sought emergency contraception after birth control failure.*

*The pharmacist called them irresponsible, refused to fill the prescription, and did not enter it into the system so that it could be transferred elsewhere."* Gretchen Borchelt, "Pharmacists Can't Be Allowed to Deny Women Emergency Contraception," <u>U.S. News and World Report</u>, October 15, 2012.

Before finishing with the discussion on birth control, the impact on the disadvantaged should be mentioned. The poor, who often are assumed to all be on welfare, are the ones who need free and easy access to safe birth control. *"As the Associated Press reminds us, poor women are 'far more likely to have an unplanned pregnancy than their wealthier counterparts.'... The project [Washington University of St. Louis study] gave free birth control to more than 9,000 local women and girls, many of whom were poor or uninsured, and tracked them for two years. There were 6.3 births per 1,000 teenagers in the study group, compared to the 2010 national rate of 34 per 1,000."* Erika Eichelberger, "Shocker: Free Birth Control Means Fewer Abortions," <u>Mother Jones</u>, October 5, 2012. Free birth control means the poor are less of a burden on the welfare system; the uninsured aren't suffering delivery costs or risky home births, and teenagers on birth control are able to get training or finish an education and find employment. For this segment of society, birth control is a win–win proposition.

But the religio-political agenda has successfully used the same tactics they have utilized in attempting to eliminate abortion. First, they restrict access as much as possible, such as removing all funding for Planned Parenthood, which helps the poor receive contraception. Secondly, they drive up the financial costs whenever they can, which is the real reason why fully covered birth control under insurance infuriates them so much. The other side to strategically raising costs would be to funnel money to anti-contraception groups for their efforts. Thirdly, they desire to reshape the Supreme Court with anti-contraception proponents to avoid another Griswold vs. Connecticut case undermining their efforts. The Religious Right wants to populate the court with extremists like themselves.

Why is a woman's access to a doctor-prescribed medication dependent upon anybody's personal opinion under the guise of his or her conscience in the first place? This is not religious liberty, but elevating some people's opinion over a woman's because she does not conform to their standard. This relegates a woman and her personal choices, in her private life, as open for debate by those deemed more worthy or more valuable -- thus judging women's decision-making as needing censure, correction, and controlling. Women's autonomy is under attack, make no mistake. How much longer can women be masters of their own destiny if birth control is successfully cut off?

"*Trying to control reproduction has been a human activity from as far back as historians can trace it.*" Linda Gordon, _The Moral Property of Women: A History of Birth Control Politics in America_, University of Illinois Press, 2002.

# Conclusion

We have looked at several sides to the legal challenges against providing free birth control, from the reinforcement of Citizens United by giving an employer First Amendment rights, to the tactics used to control and frame the argument to their advantage, to the dangerous legal precedent that could be set if religious exemptions from laws are allowed, to how women's rights are overruled by nearly anyone's conscience. The Catholic Church has a long history of being against abortion, before the evangelicals got into the game. The Church has forbidden birth control, and even vasectomies, for a long while. If this truly is about their conscience as a faith-based employer, why did they turn on their own doctrine when it benefited them?

When St. Thomas More hospital in Cañon City Colorado, run by Catholic Health

Initiatives, received a wrongful death lawsuit over the death of Lori Stodghill and her unborn twin boys, the Church's legal defense maintained the wrongful death charges only applied to "born alive" persons, not to the two unborn fetuses. Once this legal defense made international news, St. Thomas More hospital changed their defense strategy. It appears that even their own conscience shifts if it lessens their liability. The state Supreme Court will soon decide if they will hear the case.

This certainly makes it appear that the Catholic Church uses issues to benefit themselves, and thus the birth control coverage issue could be more about what they could gain in this case. As we have discussed, an exemption from a federal law for religious reasons will be felt in many, many ways and areas. Ultimately, it benefits the church to be above the law, and birth control coverage may be the issue they can easily use to achieve such an exemption. They have manufactured an issue that, in light of their Lori Stodghill wrongful death defense, they don't seem to feel that their conscience is burdened over the twins' deaths.

The only reason to manipulate and manufacture an issue is for control of women or to establish a legal precedent, or both. Is the Catholic Church dictating no birth control coverage because women have taken it in spite of the Church's stance, thus forcing women to comply? Or is this a bid for religious supremacy over the nation's laws?

Ultimately, though, this is a widespread attack on women's progress and rights, and the conscience of a few weighing more than the rights of all women is contributing to the reversal of women's advances. Again, Quiverfull can take considerable, but dubious, credit for this societal change towards women and the about-face in turning birth control from a great liberator, to a "slut-maker."

How do you force a vision of women's domestic role in this "post feminist" age? Throughout this work, we have seen a "traditional" vision of women being forced and controlled, primarily by removing what has allowed women to enter the workforce, get higher educations, and control their own destinies -- by restricting access to birth control. Beyond the information covered in this writing, we see evidence of societal pressure on women to direct all their energies on having and raising babies in the "Mommy Wars" phenomenon, combined with the unrelenting pressure on childfree adults to have children. We see all of these forces in full-swing today, and yet some women don't see the writing on the wall.

## Read all about the Religious Right with this book.

This work is a timely exposé of the Religious Right that gives insights into the Religious Right network's blueprint for America -- from Christian Reconstructionists, Dominionists, Quiverfull, the Seven Mountains Mandate, to the war on women, and attacks on public schools. Find out who the leaders of the movement are, and their tactics.

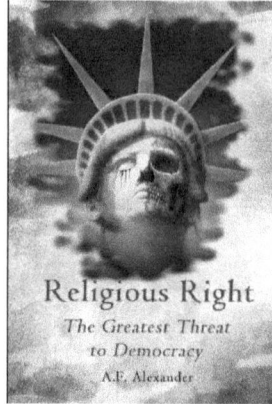

Religious Right
The Greatest Threat
to Democracy
A.F. Alexander

Book endorsement:

*"Every freedom-loving American should read this book. A.F. Alexander lays out the facts as only an insider could, and they are startling. Christian Dominionism represents a clear and present danger to our democracy, and this book tells you what each of us can do to protect the liberty we all hold so dear."* Jason Childs, founder of the Center for Progress in Alabama, Liberty University graduate, and former evangelical Baptist pastor.

## Barnes & Noble Anonymous Reviewer 5 Stars

*"I couldn't put it down. This book ties together all the pieces of the pervasive Dominionist movement. Theocrats really are systematically gaining control of the 'seven mountains' of our society."*

## Amazon Reviewer Ronald Maron (Nova Scotia) 5 Stars

*"In a clearly defined and fluid manner, the author defines the Seven Mountains of Influence, which serves as the blueprint for a religious based government, the leading protagonists behind this movement and the length and breadth to which it has already succeeded."*

www.ingramcontent.com/pod-product-compliance
Lightning Source LLC
Chambersburg PA
CBHW060703030426
42337CB00017B/2733